Contents

Introduction

Knowing the best and easiest ways to use dynamic digital resources helps teachers and students alike thrive in today's classroom. It's possible, however, that a new piece of equipment has shown up in your classroom, and you are watching it gather dust. Perhaps you feel overwhelmed by the sheer variety of technology at hand or are unsure what students and other educators are talking about. It's really impossible to ignore technology in the 21st century. *Teaching With Wikis, Blogs, Podcasts & More* aims to boost your confidence in using technology. Throughout this book, you will find straightforward and practical ideas that show you ways to integrate the most current digital resources with your daily instruction to spark student learning.

How to Use This Book

Teaching With Wikis, Blogs, Podcasts & More is divided into eight key areas, covering basics, wikis and blogs, interactives, presentation software, LCD/book projectors, audio and visual recording, and publishing student work. You can use these chapters and lessons in any order. Since each one stands alone, pick and choose based on your needs. You'll discover ways to guide students through a productive Web search, innovative methods to publish student work, strategies for effective classroom management, and more.

All activities are broken down into simple, step-by-step instructions. Some are supported with reproducibles to stretch students' understanding. The book is peppered with fun facts to share with your students and tips to aid you. After working through the initial lessons and trying some of the additional activities, you'll soon be comfortable enough to dive into the Ideas for Future Lessons. Ultimately, this book will help you view technology not only as a tool you can use to enhance your teaching but also to motivate your students and keep them on task and learning.

A Special Note About Privacy, Safety, and Permission

When students are posting information or communicating via the Internet, remind them to avoid providing personal information. Privacy settings are available. You should check your school policies before allowing students to freely use wikis, blogs, social networking, or other forms of communication. In addition, your school may have an official Internet-related permission form for you to use. If not, you'll find a reproducible permission form on page 48. Feel free to adapt it to suit your needs. Whichever form you use, be sure to have parents review the permission request and indicate which activities they agree to have their child participate in.

Teaching With
Wikis, Blogs, Podcasts & More

Kathleen Fitzgibbon

NEW YORK • TORONTO • LONDON • AUCKLAND • SYDNEY
MEXICO CITY • NEW DELHI • HONG KONG • BUENOS AIRES

Teaching *Resources*

With special thanks to Dianne Murray, contributing writer,

Grade 5 teacher, Austin Independent School District.

Scholastic Inc. grants teachers permission to photocopy the reproducible pages from this book for classroom use. No other part of this publication may be reproduced in whole or in part, or stored in a retrieval system, or transmitted in any form or by any means, electronic, mechanical, photocopying, recording, or otherwise, without written permission of the publisher. For information regarding permission, write to Scholastic Inc., 557 Broadway, New York, NY 10012.

Editor: Mela Ottaiano
Cover by Brian LaRossa
Interior design by Kathy Massaro

ISBN-13: 978-0-545-16834-2
ISBN-10: 0-545-16834-1

Copyright © 2010 by Kathleen Fitzgibbon
All rights reserved.
Printed in the U.S.A.
Published by Scholastic Inc.

2 3 4 5 6 7 8 9 10   40   16 15 14 13 12 11 10

Basics

Introduction to E-mail

Even though e-mail went widely public in the early 1990s, there are many students who have never sent an e-mail. This lesson is an introduction to e-mail that allows students to write and send their own e-mail.

Materials

* Annotated e-mail (page 11)
* Visual presenter with an LCD projector or overhead projector
* Classroom computer

Fun Facts

> The *e* in e-mail means *electronic*.

> Ray Tomlinson sent the first e-mail in 1971.

> The word *e-mail* is used as a noun, an adjective, and a verb.

> *Spam* isn't just canned meat; it's unsolicited e-mail, or junk mail. The name was inspired from a Monty Python skit.

Fun Facts

> CC stands for *carbon copy*. In the days before photocopying and electronic documents, people made copies by putting a sheet of carbon paper between two or more sheets of regular paper. Text was typed or written on the original top page. The pressure on the carbon paper created a copy on the sheet of paper directly underneath. These were called carbon copies and abbreviated *cc*. CC is still used in e-mails and business letters, though the copies are no longer made using carbon paper.

> BCC stands for *blind carbon copy*. When using this function, those people receiving the e-mail can't see who the other recipients are.

Procedure

1. Provide each student with a blank e-mail form (page 11).

2. Project the diagram of an e-mail.

3. Identify and explain the parts of an e-mail.

4. Have volunteers come up to the visual presenter and fill in the appropriate information in each part.

5. Have each student write an e-mail to a friend that tells how to write an e-mail.

Additional Activities

Provide the following prompt for students.

❋ A local travel agency is holding an online contest to give away a dream vacation. To enter you must write an e-mail to the travel agent detailing your dream trip. Make sure your e-mail includes everywhere you want to go. Is this a tour of several countries, a beach destination, or an outdoor adventure? Include the activities you'd like to do and food you'd like to eat. Don't forget to tell the travel agent how you'd like to travel—by plane, ship, train, or tour bus.

❋ Have students write their dream vacation e-mail on a classroom computer and send it to the teacher. (The teacher must have a classroom e-mail account. E-mail accounts can be set up with any free Internet service provider.)

✳ Have students complete the Venn diagram on page 12 to compare and contrast e-mail and traditional mail delivery. Have them write a persuasive paragraph on which is better.

Tips

> Most e-mails contain double spaces between paragraphs instead of indentions.

> E-mails are generally shorter than traditional letters and more to the point.

> Always use spell-check before sending an e-mail.

Ideas for Future Lessons

✳ Send e-mails with photographs

✳ Send e-mails with attachments

✳ Set up a personal e-mail account

✳ Reply to a letter sent by the teacher

✳ Create a signature line

Search Engines

Tips

> Search for a phrase or a proper name to narrow results. Remember, be specific!

> Use double quotes (" ") around a phrase when you want to search for the exact words in that exact order.

> Pay attention to spelling, spacing, and syntax to get the results you want. However, capitalization doesn't matter.

> Avoid homophones. The computer doesn't know if you mean China (country) or china (dishes).

> Most search engines assume you mean "and/or" when searching for two nouns. Use *and* (or the symbols + or &) when combining two topics (*tigers* and *India* will get results of tigers specifically in India). Use *or* with synonyms or to broaden a search (*hurricane* or *typhoon* will get results that tell the differences between the two, as well as information on worldwide tropical storms). If you are getting too many sites, add more terms and the word *and*. If the selection is too narrow, remove some terms, change terms, change *and* to *or*.

> With fewer search terms, you usually get more sites in your search.

A search engine is a software program that looks for Web sites sorted by the topic you are searching for. There are a lot of search engines. Descriptions of search engines and their uses are available on several Web sites—search for them! Many search engines are made specifically for children. Your school district may have ones that it recommends you to use.

Introduction to Searching

Materials

* Classroom computer

* Whiteboard or other device to project screen for class to see

Procedure

1. Brainstorm with students possible topics for writing a report. Make sure at least one of their topics is too broad. (For example, *Mississippi*.)

2. Demonstrate how to type the topic in the search engine search box.

3. Point out the number of results. (*Mississippi* garnered more than 100 million sites!)

4. Discuss with students ways to narrow their search by clarifying what they want to know. (*Mississippi River* narrowed it to about 20 million sites.) Continue to narrow the topic and let students see the changes in the number of sites. (*History of Mississippi River* narrowed to about 400,000; *history of Mississippi River during Civil War* narrowed to about 190,000.) Seeing thousands of sites may feel overwhelming. Instruct students to just look at the first 20 or so in the list. If you don't see what you're looking for, narrow the topic some more.

5. Once you have narrowed down your search, show how each site has a title and a brief description. Instruct students to read the description before clicking the title to save themselves the time of opening sites they cannot use. Display sites and show how to go back to the search list.

Identifying Types of Web Sites

1. Suggest a search topic that will elicit both reliable and unreliable Web sites, such as, *Saturn, tiger,* or *cardinals.*

2. Have pairs or groups of students make four-column charts and label the columns *.org, .gov, .com,* and *other.* Have students sort the Web sites they find into the four categories. *Other* might include *.net, .edu,* or even sites based in other countries, such as *.uk* or *.ca.*

3. Have students look at two Web sites from each column and make notes giving brief descriptions of each.

4. Have students make generalizations about each kind of URL. Discuss which sites are most reliable for doing school research.

Fun Facts

> A URL, or Uniform Resource Locator, is a Web site address.

> TinyURL is a service that allows users to shorten a long URL, making it easier to remember or retype.

Choosing Reliable Web Sites

* The last three letters of a URL tell what kind of Web site it is. Students should typically use these types of sites for research purposes:

  * *.gov* sites are hosted by the government;
  * *.edu* sites are hosted by schools;
  * *.org* sites are organizations, mainly not-for-profit organizations. Museums and libraries usually end in *.org.*

* Does the URL contain a tilde (~)? Beware of addresses with a tilde. That means that though it is a part of the initial site address (even with an *.edu,* associated with a university), it was not created, published, or maintained by the initial site. For example, it may be a Web page created by a university student.

* A common Web site ending is *.com.* These sites often have a commercial purpose. Students should take this into consideration when using information found here.

Tips

> The editors of *Instructor* magazine maintain a Web site with language arts, social studies, science, and sports and hobby CyberHunts. These include questions, Web sites, and answers. The Web site is http://teacher.scholastic.com/products/instructor/cyberhunt_kids.htm.

> Set up a style for how Web sites are documented as sources in student papers. The MLA style lists:

  - author's last name, first name;
  - quotation marks around the article title;
  - main name of Web site;
  - date article was read and used;
  - URL address set in angle brackets (< >).

If the Web site doesn't indicate an author, begin the citation with the name of the article in quotation marks.

Scavenger Hunts

Scavenger hunts are a fun way for students to learn how to navigate a Web site and do online research.

1. Create an online scavenger hunt. You will have to practice the hunt before you assign it to be sure that all Web sites are safe and reliable. Begin by choosing a topic that you are studying in the classroom.

2. Create a list of questions and provide the URL students will use to answer them. All questions may be from one URL, or you may send students to several different Web sites. Steer students to reliable Web sites, such as national parks, government agencies, and public television.

3. Working in pairs or individually, have students find and write answers to the questions.

4. Provide an answer key so students can check their own work.

Parts of an E-mail

Send **Attach** **Fonts** **Save as Draft**

From:

To:

CC:

BCC:

Subject:

From or Account: sender's e-mail account name

This is seen in e-mails you receive, not in e-mails you send.

To: e-mail address of who is receiving the e-mail

CC: other people you are sending e-mail to

Used for additional e-mail addresses. Everyone who receives the e-mail can see these addresses.

BCC: other people you are sending e-mail to

Used for additional e-mail addresses. People who receive e-mail cannot see these addresses.

Subject: a line or a couple of words describing the message's topic

Message Body: area to write the e-mail, similar to the body of a letter

Be sure to include a:

* **Greeting:** such as *Dear, Hello,* or *Hi*

* **Closing:** a word or two ending the e-mail, such as *Sincerely* or *Yours Truly*

* **Signature Line:** your name

Teaching With Wikis, Blogs, Podcasts & More © 2010 by Kathleen Fitzgibbon, Scholastic Teaching Resources

Name _____ Date _____

E-mail vs. U.S. Mail

Complete a Venn diagram to compare and contrast e-mail and the U.S. mail (sometimes referred to now as "snail mail"). After completing the diagram, write a short paragraph telling which form of communication is better and why.

E-mail   **U.S. Mail**

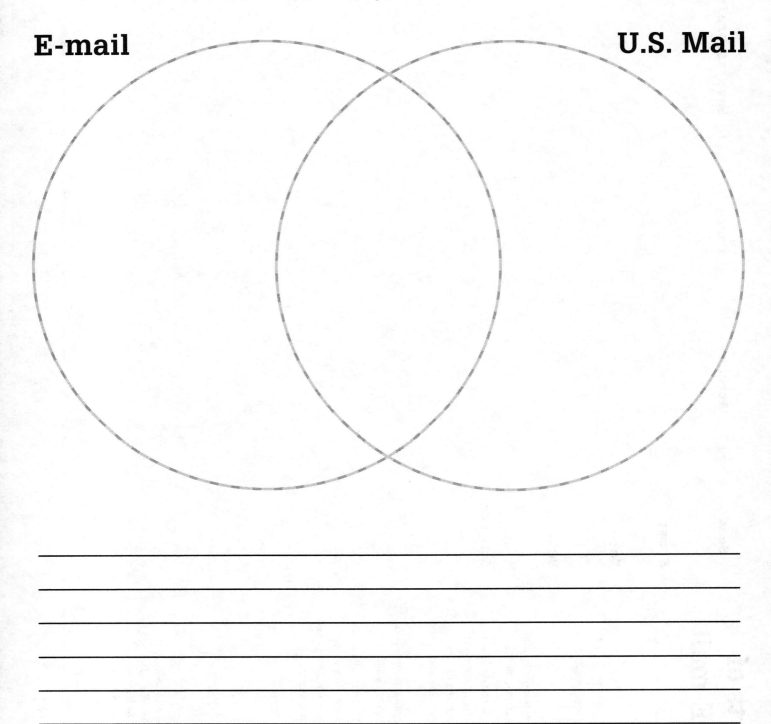

_____

_____

_____

_____

_____

Teaching With Wikis, Blogs, Podcasts & More © 2010 by Kathleen Fitzgibbon, Scholastic Teaching Resources

Wikis and Blogs

Think of a blog as an individual's online journal and a wiki as an open forum for a community to share ideas about a particular topic. Both formats have grown in popularity because of their ease of use and the number of free software options offered on the Internet since the late 1990s.

A typical blogger (person who blogs) writes about any number of subjects, like a hobby or personal observations and then posts the writing (or blog) to the Internet. People who read the blog can post comments about the blog's content, and then the blogger can comment on those comments, starting a dialogue. Typically, a blog post is at the top of the page and underneath it are the reader's comments followed by the blogger's responses. The actual blog or comments can only be edited by the blogger and not by the other contributors.

A wiki is similar to a blog in that both center around hobbies, life experiences, political, or academic subjects, but a wiki offers versatility. A wiki is a Web site that uses wiki software that allows for the easy creation and editing of interlinked Web pages. They are a democratic way to share and create content. Wikis, comprised of Web pages, can be edited, deleted, or created by anyone who visits (or *migrates*) to the wiki. The participatory nature of a wiki makes the experience nonlinear, as users hop, skip, and click to retrieve or contribute information.

Create a Wiki

Students create a wiki that serves as a way to post homework assignments and notices to parents, and also serves as a classroom community resource.

Fun Facts

> Wiki means "quick" or "fast" in Hawaiian, like the Wiki Wiki airport shuttle in Honolulu. Wiki edits post almost immediately.

> Wikipedia is probably the most well-known wiki. It's a free encyclopedia project based mostly on anonymous contributions. Wikipedia is written by a group of volunteers but anyone can access the text and write or make changes to its articles.

Materials

❋ Computer with Internet access

❋ Scanner

Procedure

1. Begin by guiding students on tours of different wikis you find online. Help students not only to become confident navigating wikis but also to gather ideas for setting up their own.

2. Use an online search engine to locate free resources to set up a wiki. Some wiki Web sites only require you to name your wiki and create a URL. Don't be intimidated by the sound of a URL; it's just the wiki's address on the Internet. Other sites require only a user name and password. This process takes five to ten minutes.

3. Create categories within the wiki. These are areas that you want your students either to glean information from, participate in, or contribute content to.

   Category suggestions:

   ● **Assignments** Post homework on a calendar that serves as an online check-in for parents and students to see assignments and when they are due.

   ● **Reading lists** Post a list of recommended books in different genres.

   ● **Online novels or e-books** You and students suggest Web sites that have complete novels, graphic novels, short stories, and plays.

   ● **List of local libraries** Many libraries offer computers and online services at no cost, providing a free resource for students without computers. Remember to add links to online maps showing the librarys' locations.

- **Writers' corner** This is a place for students to post their homework or creative content in folders.

- **Partners in writing** These are hubs where groups of children write and edit short stories, plays, or novels.

- **Book club discussion** Students add comments or suggestions about books they have read or other students have read. Students can also design a book cover, photograph it, and then upload it to the wiki to create an enticing blurb. Students can elaborate and discuss a book's plot, theme, or characters.

4. In addition, send home a letter that includes the wiki Web address and instructions for parents to contribute to the site.

5. Teach students proper wiki etiquette. Check the wiki regularly to be sure users are following proper etiquette. (See *Wiki and Blog Etiquette*, at right.)

Additional Activities

❋ Lead a discussion about how the word *post* is used both as a verb and a noun online.

❋ Students interview local authors and post the interviews to a literature wiki.

❋ Post publicity shots of special projects on a classroom wiki.

Ideas for Future Lessons

❋ Create a virtual museum wiki about art and the people who work in museums. Develop an art show, from concept to the opening. An art exhibit is a collaborative process, just like a wiki experience. Students research everyone from directors to docents to gallery assistants. Students make their own art to photograph or scan, and then upload to the wiki.

❋ Have students create a wiki based on an ancient civilization's culture and society. Encourage them to use the Wiki Web Organizer (page 19) to categorize subject matter on the wiki.

Wiki and Blog Etiquette

❋ No cursing. No slang.

❋ No name calling.

❋ Write in complete sentences. Use capitalization and punctuation. Spell correctly.

❋ Do not write in ALL CAPS. It is considered shouting.

❋ Keep it brief.

❋ Give praise when due.

❋ Argue facts, not personalities.

❋ Post small photos; they download quickly.

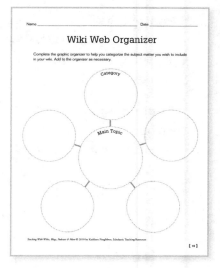

Create a Blog

Encourage students to pick an area of personal interest, such as soccer, movies, ballet, or astronomy. Then they set up their own blog, and write at least one post each week.

Materials

❋ Computer with Internet access

Procedure

1. Assist students with selecting a subject that will remain interesting over time. Compare it to writing a research paper or keeping a journal.

2. Have students go online and find a free software tool for creating blogs. They name their blogs and create a blog address or URL. Encourage students to make the title catchy.

3. Have students choose a template, a tool that creates the page where they write and categorizes content.

4. Have students write their first blog posting. As students gain experience and refine their topics, they may add other features. (See *Parts of a Blog* on page 17.). Encourage students to post photographs to enhance and personalize their blogs.

5. Assign students to read other classmate's blogs and post comments. Remind them to follow blog etiquette. (See *Wiki and Blog Etiquette* on page 15.) If your school doesn't already have an official policy, be sure to let students know an important rule: Keep personal information private. Do not post it on an Internet site.

Types of Blogs

❋ **Vlogs**
a video blog made of short video clips

❋ **Photoblogs**
content consists mainly of photographs rather than text

❋ **Audio blogs**
a blog of audio files instead of text

Additional Activities

✳ Have students add an "about me" sidebar that is a short biography.

✳ Lead a class discussion about blog design and creating visual interest. Have students work in pairs examining various blogs, listing the features they find appealing and incorporating some of the features into their own blogs.

✳ Invite students to research other blogs based on particular subject, pick their favorites, and then add links to their blogs.

Ideas for Future Lessons

✳ Instruct students to blog about different infectious diseases throughout history. They can create links to the Center for Disease Control, emergency agencies, and appropriate government sites.

✳ Assign small groups of students to take turns being class reporters. They should maintain a daily blog about classroom "news."

✳ Invite students to create a classroom gardener's blog documenting the process of planting and caring for a garden. If possible, have them incorporate video, photographs, and audio.

✳ Have students write a blog about the school's neighborhood that includes local residents, area activities, and history. Take them on a walking tour so they can photograph interesting people or sites that make the area unique. Then students will write captions for the photos and essays about their experiences. Send the Web address to your school's parent community coordinator so the observations can be shared with the community.

Parts of a Blog

✳ **Header** — Name of blog and a brief description

✳ **Post** — An entry, also called an article, about the selected subject

✳ **Post/Article Title** — The "headline" for your post. Remember to make it catchy to draw attention to your article.

✳ **Search** — Function that allows a user to locate specific content within the blog posts

✳ **Archives** — A list of entries usually arranged by month and year in reverse chronological order

✳ **Comments** — A place where readers comment on the blog

✳ **Favorite Links** — Highlighted words that, when clicked, take readers to linked Web sites

✳ **Sidebar** — An area beside the main blog that contains information that enhances the main blog, often points of interest bloggers want to share with readers

Wikis vs. Blogs

Have students complete a Venn diagram to compare and contrast blogs and wikis. (See page 20.) After completing the diagram, students locate an example of each online and explain to the class what they like about both formats.

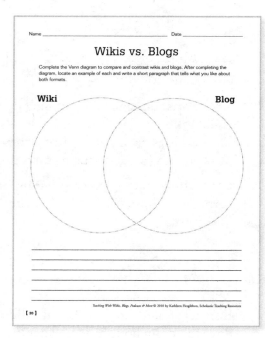

Social Networking Sites

Social networking sites, such as Facebook and MySpace, are places where individuals build a personal space on the Web. They then invite others to be their friends. They share information, common interests, photographs, and communicate with one another on these sites.

Another social networking and blogging site is Twitter. To communicate, users send "tweets." A tweet is a 140-character message sent to specific people on the network. A user must be at least 13 years old to use this network.

Because of the personal nature of these sites, many schools have banned their use or blocked access altogether. Web sites and articles are available with instruction on teaching students how to use social networking sites safely and with appropriate etiquette. Check your school's policies.

Name _____ Date _____

Wiki Web Organizer

Complete the graphic organizer to help you categorize the subject matter you wish to include in your wiki. Add to the organizer as necessary.

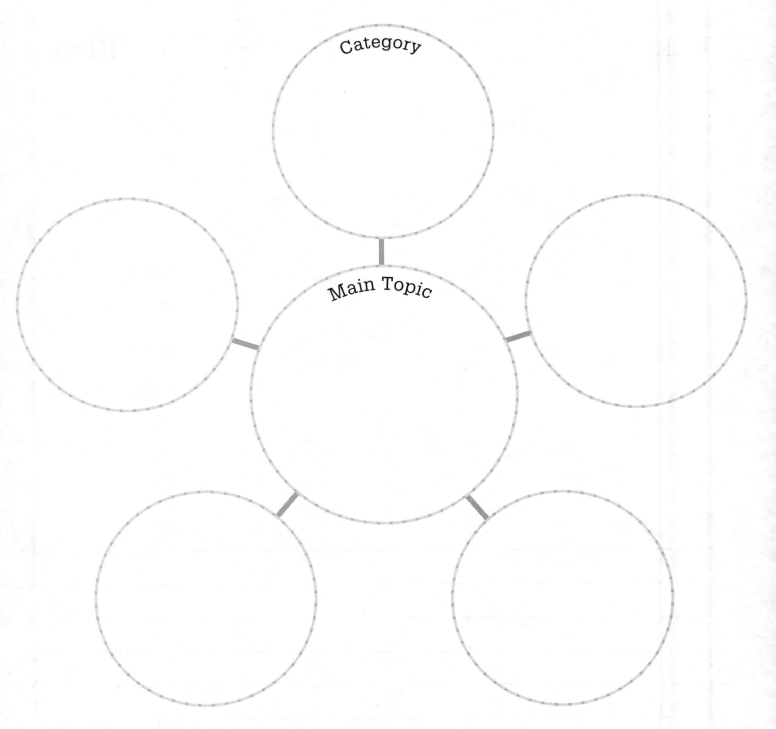

Wikis vs. Blogs

Complete the Venn diagram to compare and contrast wikis and blogs. After completing the diagram, locate an example of each and write a short paragraph that tells what you like about both formats.

Wiki
Blog

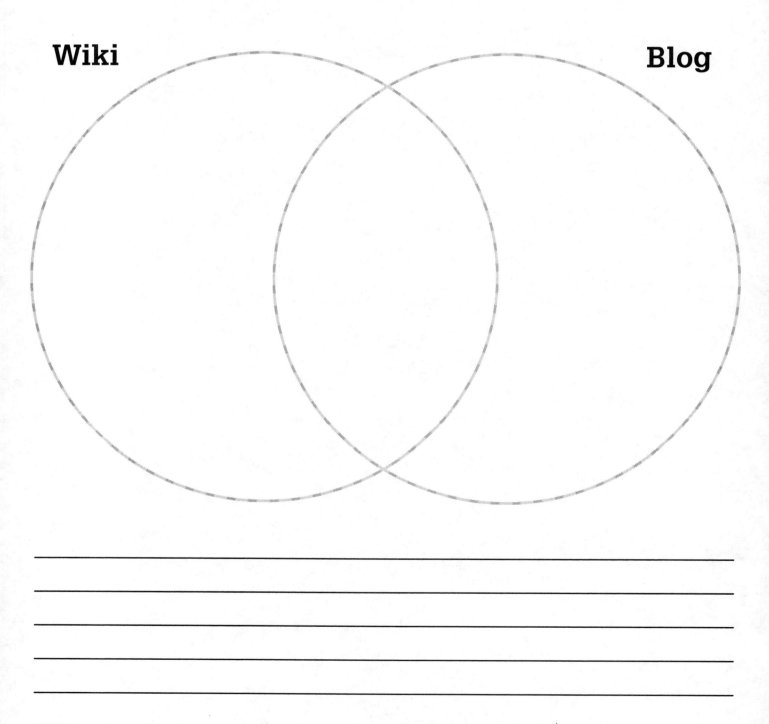

_____

_____

_____

_____

_____

Interactives

▶ **Interactive Whiteboards**

I nteractive whiteboards take the place of chalkboards, traditional dry-erase boards, or chart tablets. Anything that can be seen on a computer desktop can be displayed on an interactive whiteboard. The whiteboard screen works just like a computer desktop, with pull-down menus, tools, multiple files, etc. Unlike a traditional chalkboard, all instruction (including any annotations) can be saved.

Ways to Reuse
Recorded
Instruction

✻ with students who
were absent during
initial presentation

✻ with students who
benefit from repetition

✻ with struggling learners

✻ as a pretest review

Using an Interactive Whiteboard

To help students understand the capabilities of the interactive whiteboard, have groups plan presentations.

Materials

✻ Interactive whiteboard

✻ Computer

✻ Research materials (nonfiction books, encyclopedias, Internet access)

Procedure

1. Divide students into two groups and assign each a research topic related to your classroom study.

2. Instruct students to carry out the research and plan how they will make multimedia presentations to the class. Have one group plan to use traditional materials, such as poster board, photographs, and paper resources. Have the other group plan to use the computer and interactive whiteboard.

3. If time permits, let students complete their presentations. If not, just have students plan what they will do but not carry it out.

4. Let each group make (or explain) its presentations to the class.

5. Together with students, complete two-column charts on the pros and cons of each type of presentation. During the discussion, demonstrate the features of the interactive whiteboard.

Tools

✳ Record everything that happens on the whiteboard. The built-in recorder lets you record audio through a microphone and automatically combines audio and data into one file for playback on any computer.

✳ Make annotations at the top of a video.

✳ Highlighter, screen pointer, spotlight, and other key functions are available in the toolbar.

✳ Write and draw on the whiteboard as you would a chalkboard. Then pick up and move, resize, or save what you wrote.

✳ Connect a DVD or VHS player to the projector to display movies on the whiteboard.

Ways to Use an Interactive Whiteboard in Your Classroom

✳ **Multimedia Presentations** Both teachers and students can present multimedia projects, controlling the entire presentation without using a computer keyboard.

✳ **Video** Video clips can be embedded within a multimedia presentation. On the whiteboard, videos can be paused, highlighted, circled, annotated, etc.

✳ **Notes** Anything written on the whiteboard can be printed and saved.

Notes can be
  - saved in a file for reuse at a later presentation,
  - downloaded by students,
  - posted on a Web page or blog,
  - printed out and distributed.

✳ **Critical Thinking** Use an outline format to organize classroom brainstorming. Concept-mapping software can be projected and used to record student ideas. Graphic organizers can be completed as a group and saved for future use.

✳ **Special Needs Students** Interactive whiteboards allow the use of large fonts and bright colors. Students can respond simply by touching the board.

Teaching Ideas

✳ Digital storytelling

✳ Annotating student multimedia presentations

✳ Using online map and satellite imagery

✳ Labeling parts of artwork or online museum presentations

✳ Demonstrating movie-making techniques, keyboard techniques, software, and other computer skills

✳ Saving diagrams of plays or techniques for sports or physical education activities

✳ Collaborating on writing/editing and math examples

✳ Documenting science experiments

✳ Electronic word wall

Tips

> CRS is best used for true/false, multiple-choice, or short answers (numeral, one word, or phrase).

> Individualize and differentiate instruction using the graphed results.

> Gives shy students a chance to respond without having to speak in front of the class.

> Students can view questions on the remote control LCD screen displayed by the teacher or read aloud by the teacher.

Classroom Response System

A classroom response system (CRS) provides each student with a remote control that students can use to answer a question. All of the student responses are recorded on a computer. Responses can immediately be shown in a graph.

Classroom Management

Pretest Procedure

1. As students enter the class, have them immediately pick up their assigned remote control devices.

2. Let students answer programmed questions displayed in the device or project questions you have prepared using presentation software.

3. When students are done, display the graph for each response that shows how many students got it correct. Discuss the answer to each question.

4. In the whole-class setting, individual responses remain private. However, you will be able to note which students had difficulty. Plan lessons accordingly, differentiating instruction as needed.

Lecture Format Procedure

1. Begin class with 10–15 minutes of instruction. Then use the response system to assess student understanding of the material.

2. During this assessment, students may respond individually, in pairs, or in small groups. In this way, the questions may stimulate discussion and help students better understand why one response is correct.

3. Correct answers may be discussed during the assessment or after (as in the Pretest Procedure).

4. Use the question discussion and CRS responses to provide more information or adjust curriculum.

Uses for CRS

* Take attendance.

* Morning warm-up: Teacher poses a question for students to think about. They respond via the remote, and results become a class warm-up discussion.

* Record student feedback (yes/no; I like/don't like; rating on a scale).

* Students take remotes home and submit answers to homework questions. Answers are recorded as soon as students enter class.

* Student surveys: These are either teacher- or student-directed.

* Repeated questions: Students respond to a question, then discuss it with a partner or do research. To follow up, they respond a second time to the same question.

* Record classroom voting.

* Give pretests and posttests.

* View data by class or by student.

* Provide immediate feedback to students.

* Differentiate instruction and assessment.

* Unlike the traditional raising of hands, all responses are private.

Chapter 4

Presentation Software

Presentation software allows users to create slides that are projected onto a screen through a document camera or computer connected to an LCD projector.

War Correspondent

In this activity, students are war correspondents sending home news reports and commentary from a combat zone or a place of hostility. They will make a three-minute presentation to the class on a war in the time period you are studying.

Materials

❋ Presentation software

❋ Classroom computer

❋ Projection device, such as a document camera or LCD projector

❋ Screen

Name _____ Date _____
5 Ws and How
Topic: _____
Who?
What?
When?
Where?
Why?
How?
Other Notes: _____
[26]   *Teaching With Wikis, Blogs, Podcasts & More © 2010 by Kathleen Neughboen, Scholastic Teaching Resources*

Procedure

1. Remind students that all news reporting begins and ends with the "5 Ws and H": *Who, What, When, Where, Why, How.* (See page 28.)

2. Brainstorm with students general questions they will answer in their presentations.

   - *Who* were the significant leaders in the war? These could be presidents, military figures, or other key government officials.

   - *What* happened in the war?

   - *When* did the war begin and end?

   - *Where* did the war take place?

   - *Why* did the war happen?

   - *How* did the war advance? Examples include military strategies like ground or air attacks, weapons used, or diplomatic negotiations.

3. Students research to find answers to the six questions.

4. Walk students through the basics of using the presentation software. Tutorials are available online.

Teaching Uses for Presentation Software

* A variety of lessons are available online at no charge. Many come with interactive tests.

* Use a document camera or LCD projector to screen a presentation for the entire class.

* Transform an oral exam into a game-show format using presentation software.

* Use presentation software on Parent Night to explain how your grade level or classroom operates.

* Presentation software can be used in the same way you would use a flip chart.

* For information on publishing student presentations, see Chapter 8, "Publishing Student Work."

Tips

Reminders to Students

> Limit the number to 6 to 10 slides.

> Don't crowd the slide with too much text so it's easy to read from a distance.

> Font size should be 28 to 34 bold, and titles should be 44.

> Don't use too many fonts. Graphics and design capabilities are built into the software.

> Light type on dark background or dark type on light background display the best.

> Proofread the slides. Make sure the slides are in the correct order.

> Use transitions between slides. Transitions are available in the software.

> Incorporate sound and audio. Be creative: record your own music onto the computer. Any music on your computer can be imported into the presentation.

> Use maps, photographs, graphs, diagrams, clip art, or video.

> Slides can also be used for Webcasts.

Name _____ Date _____

5 Ws and How

Topic: _____

Who?

What?

When?

Where?

Why?

How?

Other Notes: _____

_____

_____

LCD/Book Projectors

Anything placed under the camera lens of a visual projector (or document camera) can be projected onto a screen, whiteboard, or wall. The technology provides the ability to switch back and forth between viewing a hard copy document, accessing presentation software, playing an instructional video, and viewing a document stored on the computer. Teachers can demonstrate three-dimensional objects or display text and maps for the whole class to see. A microscope feature can even be added to the presenter to display information at a microscopic level.

Editing/Proofreading

Materials

❉ Visual presenter/document camera connected to an LCD projector

❉ Classroom computer with a writing program that has a grammar and spell-check tool

❉ An unedited short story and an edit symbols chart stored on the computer

❉ Felt-tip pen

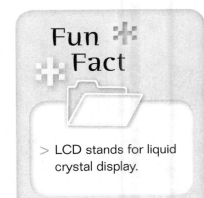

Fun Fact

> LCD stands for liquid crystal display.

Tips

> To prevent glare, avoid using white paper under the lens. Light green or blue paper creates less glare. Sometimes turning off the lights reduces the glare on documents.

> Use a laser pointer to point out details on the screen.

> Avoid ballpoint pens. Print using a thick felt pen because the projected line is easier to see.

Procedure

1. Display the short story on the screen and have students read it silently.

2. Discuss the story and have students identify errors in the story. Let volunteers come up to the camera and make editorial notes directly onto the story text using editing symbols. As needed, switch the camera from document to desktop and display the edit symbol chart.

3. Conduct a second edit of the story by running the grammar- and spell-check tool. Compare the students' edits with the software edit. (Remember, there are often discrepancies regarding software grammar and spelling suggestions. These differences create an opportunity to discuss various editing solutions.)

4. Have students individually rewrite the edited version of the story.

Ideas for Future Lessons

❋ Study gemstones using the microscope feature.

❋ Track animal migrations using maps.

❋ Display several different styles of art to compare and contrast.

Chapter  6

Audio

 Podcasts

Podcasts are audio or video broadcasts of digital media files downloaded from the Internet to computers and MP3 players for rebroadcast. Podcasts on many subjects are available free.

Create a Podcast

Materials

❋ External microphone or built-in computer microphone

❋ Software to create sound files (available free on the Internet)

❋ Podcast hosting service (also available free)

Procedure

1. Together with students, write a script. A script might be based on a topic like taking care of a class pet. The script would introduce the pet, explain the history of how your class acquired it, and discuss how students care for the pet.

Fun Facts

> An MP3 player is a device that stores, plays, and organizes audio files.

> Merriam-Webster definition:
MP3—"a computer file format for the compression and storage of digital *audio* data"

Tips

2. Let students practice reading the script several times before recording.

3. Record the broadcast using either the computer's built-in microphone or an external microphone connected to the computer. Use audio software that has the capability to create MP3 audio files. Free software is available for recording and editing voices, music, and sounds. Use the software tutorials to become familiar with its functions.

4. Link the podcast to a class wiki, blog, or online music store. You do not have to pay to upload your show, nor do others have to pay to download the program.

Publish the Podcast

1. Go to any free online server that provides a server for uploading audio files. Create a screen name and password. Some sites create your Web address using your screen name.

2. Many sites ask for a description of the podcast. Writing the description is a good lesson on summarizing. Once the podcast is uploaded to a server, this description informs listeners of your show's content or category.

3. Upload the audio file to the podcast-hosting server. It is now available to be downloaded and listened to by family members, pen pals, other students, and anyone interested in the subject.

Ideas for Future Lessons

These ideas focus on using a computer's internal microphone and audio software.

✳ Students build fluency by recording a reading passage and timing themselves. The student rereads the same passage until acceptable fluency is reached. Students keep a reading log listing their passages and reading rates.

✳ Readers theater classes can take advantage of the editing resources on audio software to enhance their shows by adding sound effects and manipulating voice levels and intonations in order to produce more professional broadcasts.

How to Use MP3s

MP3 players allow students to work on projects individually or at home. Although the following activities can be done on the computer, an MP3 player's portability allows for more flexibility on where the student works.

✳ Have students read and record their own writing. They can use either the computer's built-in microphone or an external microphone connected to the computer. It is also necessary to use audio software that has the ability to create MP3 files. Free software is available for recording and editing voices, music, and other sounds. Be sure to take advantage of the software tutorials to become familiar with its functions.

✳ Invite students to listen to foreign language podcasts. They can then practice the language by recording and listening to themselves speak.

✳ Famous historical speeches are available for downloading. Let students listen to the speech individually or as part of a class homework assignment.

✳ Music lessons can be downloaded so students can play along with their instruments.

Benefits of Audiobooks

✳ Use audiobooks in reading centers or for after-school book clubs.

✳ Students can follow along with audiobooks using a hard copy of the book.

✳ The whole class can listen to an audiobook and follow up with a class discussion or group instruction on a comprehension skill.

✳ Audiobooks can level the reading field for second-language learners and struggling readers.

✳ Students actively listen by answering participatory questions that require rewinding, pausing, and replaying segments of the book. These notes prepare the students for class discussions.

✳ Students develop literacy skills by using specific lessons on vocabulary, story elements, genre, and word study.

E-books

E-books (short for *electronic books*) are conventional print books in a digital format. They can be read on computers, e-readers, or some mobile phones. A portable e-reader can hold hundreds of books in a device about the size of paperback book.

Book vs. E-book

Let students compare and contrast a conventional book with an e-book and determine the advantages and disadvantages of the e-book format. (See page 35.) Most e-books must be purchased individually. Many books that are in the public domain are available free online.

Materials

❋ Popular conventional book

❋ Download the e-book version of the same book. (Many titles, including Lewis Carroll's *Alice's Adventures in Wonderland*, are available free online.)

Procedure

1. Working in pairs or in small groups, have students read a selected passage, such as one chapter, from each version of the book.

2. Give students the following questions and have them find answers in both versions of the book. Have them record their responses on a two-column chart.

- You are in a dark room. What can you do to read the book?

- Your battery has gone dead. How can you read the book?

- How will you mark where you stopped reading?

- How can you find Alice's conversation with the Caterpillar (provide specific quote, subhead, or vocabulary word)?

- An elderly relative with poor eyesight would like to look at your book. What can you do to make the text more readable?

3. Encourage students to explore and discuss the two versions. Then have them make a list of the advantages and disadvantages of each format.

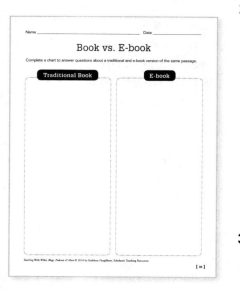

Name _____ Date _____

Book vs. E-book

Complete a chart to answer questions about a traditional and e-book version of the same passage.

Traditional Book

E-book

Chapter 7

Visual Recording

> ▶ **Digital Cameras**

Create a Class Book

Start the school year by creating a class book of information. Students will design and respond to a survey, write personal narratives, and become familiar with digital cameras. Students get to know each other better, and the book can be used to track changes.

Materials

❋ Digital camera

❋ Photo printer or good quality printer (photo printing may be done by a commercial lab)

❋ Computers, printers, paper

❋ Brads or other book binding materials; you may wish to use a three-ring binder so new students can be added.

Procedure

1. Work with students to design a survey of personal information to share in a class book. Note that this book will only be for classroom/school use. It should not be published or posted on a Web site. Help students edit the questions so as not to embarrass or shame any students. Questions may include favorites (such as food, TV show, book), sports or hobbies, an amusing memory, etc.

2. Have each student complete the survey.

3. Depending on the capabilities of students, you may wish to use the surveys or have students take information from the survey and write a personal narrative about themselves.

4. Have students edit their responses and print them on quality paper.

5. Demonstrate the basic workings of the camera, such as view finder, zoom, LCD screen, and flash. Take a photograph of each student. You may wish to take one portrait shot and one of students doing something they describe in their writing.

6. Demonstrate how to download the photographs and, working with students, edit them to the best one or two photos of each student. Print the photos.

7. Together with students, bind the photos and essays into a class book.

Ideas for Future Lessons

❋ Exchange class books with another classroom and create pen pal connections.

❋ Repeat the activity mid-year and at the end of the year to compare and contrast changes in individual students and in the class.

❋ Use the surveys to make graphs and charts as math activities. These can be done using software such as Microsoft Excel.

❋ Make other class project books by photographing artwork, science experiments, community historical sites, etc., and having students write text to accompany photographs.

Fun Facts

> A digital camera works just like a conventional camera, using lenses that focus light to create an image. In a conventional camera, the image is focused on film, while in a digital camera the image is focused onto a semiconductor device.

> **JPEG** (pronounced "jay peg") stands for Joint Photographic Experts Group. JPEG is the name of the committee that wrote the standard used for the file format. JPEG files are for color photographs. JPEG is not used for animation.

> **GIF** (pronounced "jif" or "gif") stands for Graphic Interchange Format. It is used for line drawings and black-and-white images. GIF is also used for animation.

> **PNG** (pronounced "ping") stands for Portable Network Graphics. It was designed to be used like the GIF format but provides greater depth of color. PNG is not used for animation.

Tips

Classroom Management

> Make a classroom seating chart with student names and pictures for substitute teachers.

> Create locker magnets by putting photos in simple magnetic photo frames.

> Use photos to make a monthly bulletin board highlighting special activities and accomplishments.

Tripods

> Using a tripod slows a photographer down. It is a good learning tool for a beginning photographer because it forces the photographer to look, position the tripod, look again, reposition.

> Tripods are perfect for self-portraits using a built-in timer.

> A clamp pod attaches to a camera and is then clamped onto a stationary object.

Student Photographers

Provide a camera workshop that students must take before they can individually use cameras. The class teaches proper handling and safety rules.

Materials

✳ Digital camera (always have spare batteries)

✳ Camera strap

✳ Tripod (optional)

Management

Before students can check out and use a camera, they must be licensed. Provide a short workshop for 1 to 3 students. Keep it small so you can monitor students' behavior and handling of the equipment. Make a camera license, laminate it, and attach it to a string. Students must wear the license when using the camera. Students without licenses may not use cameras.

Additional Activities

✳ Scavenger hunts. Students look for and photograph geometric shapes, plants, story ideas, art project ideas. Provide any list of objects—make some items easy to find and a few more challenging.

✳ Document field trips. Have students write captions and post them on a class Web site or a photo-sharing site as a virtual field trip.

✳ Document weather, types of clouds, ocean conditions, tidal changes, student growth.

✳ Document the growth of classroom plant or pet.

✳ Cut out photographs, glue onto craft sticks, and use as stick puppets.

✳ Make personalized thank-you notes.

✳ Attach photographs to pen pal correspondence.

✳ Include photos in reports that use presentation software or print photographs for display.

Rules for Student Photographers

* Require students to keep the camera strap over their wrists or around their necks to prevent dropping the equipment.

* Show students how to fill the frame with the subject. Instruct them to get closer or use zoom. Tell students to look in the four corners before snapping the picture.

* Discourage nonsense pictures and casual snapshots.

* Explain that students may not publish any photos online without the written permission of the subject. (This may also require parental permission.)

* Have students practice holding the camera steady. Instruct students on how to use the tripod, such as how to screw in the camera and how to extend tripod legs.

Tips

Ways to Hold the Camera Steady

> Use a tripod or clamp pod.

> Set it on a steady surface, such as a desktop.

> Hold your breath as you snap the picture. Remember, there is a delay with some digital cameras—hold your breath until the camera clicks.

Digital Moviemaking

Student Filmmakers

Have students write, shoot, direct, produce, and act in a one-minute public service announcement.

Materials

* Digital video camera
* Computer with editing software
* Music and props
* External microphone

Rules for Student Filmmakers

❋ Rule of thirds—Divide the scene or image shown on the monitor into nine equal parts by two equally spaced horizontal lines and two equally spaced vertical lines. The important parts of the composition should run along these lines.

❋ Use a tripod to prevent shaky recording.

❋ Avoid recording when cars are passing or in public spaces, like restaurants.

❋ Have at least one extra camera battery.

❋ In-camera editing— Keep scenes short so there is no need to edit on a computer.

❋ Use a USB cable to attach the camera to the computer so that students can immediately see what they just filmed.

Procedure

1. Discuss with students what a public service announcement (PSA) is. Show examples available on DVD or online.

2. Demonstrate the basic parts of the camera, such as the record button, power switch, disk compartment, battery, built-in microphone, view-finder, zoom button, LCD monitor, and tripod attachment.

3. Instruct students in basic filming techniques such as, setting the camera on a tripod and *mise-en-scène* (a French term meaning every aspect of the scene that appears on the monitor—from the actors' placement to costumes, to how the set looks with props). Instruct students to avoid zooming and panning.

4. Brainstorm ideas for a school PSA. It may be an overview of your school, an issue going on in your school (such as lunchroom behavior), or a way to improve things (such as picking up litter). Together as a class, write the script.

5. Review with students all the roles needed to make a movie: director, cinematographer, costumer, sound editor, music editor, picture editor, actors.

6. Cast and shoot the video.

7. Log the video and edit it.

8. Make a DVD of your video to give to students and parents or post it on your class Web site or blog.

Additional Activities

In place of traditional book reports, students make video presentations, such as:

❋ use puppets to interview one another about the books

❋ reenact a scene in costumes depicting the book's characters

❋ pitch the book using talking points to sell it to an audience

❋ act out a scene three different ways in three different orders

Editing Steps

1. Import video into movie software. Remember to import in short segments or clips.

2. Arrange the clips in the correct sequence on the timeline.

3. Add transitions between clips using transitions provided in the software.

4. Import music or sound effects from your computer or from the list of effects provided in the software.

5. Add titles using the palette box. At this point, effects such as zoom, fly, and bounce can be added.

6. Burn the final cut to a DVD.

Basic Camera Shots

> **Close-up**
> shot of the face to show emotions

> **Medium**
> shot of person from the waist up

> **Long**
> full-body shot

> **Wide shot**
> establishes a location

> **2-shot**
> two people in the scene

Webcams

Webcams are video-capturing cameras built into or attached to computers to transmit live images over the Internet. Webcams are also used on moving objects, such as bicycles, taxis, and boats. Webcams are set up all over the world to easily bring the world to your classroom.

View From a Webcam

Search the Internet for available Webcam feeds on some of the following subject areas:

- **Science** – farms, animal sanctuaries, zoos, animal reserves, national parks, or even in the wild; NASA offers different feeds from space

- **Social Studies** – museums, factories, all landforms, urban areas from the Eiffel Tower in Paris, France, to Fifth Avenue in New York City

- **Architecture** – castles, museums, bridges, airports

- **Transportation** – railroads, cruise ships

Video Calling is a free online program, such as Skype, that allows people to call one another anywhere in the world. Both parties must have this service and agree when to meet online. This is a great way for students to talk to other classrooms in other countries or just on the other side of town.

Procedure

1. While watching a busy market in India (or other place students are studying), have students take notes to describe the people, the food, the stores, and the kinds of transportation, or let students choose any four things they want to observe. Have them write up their observations into a descriptive passage.

2. Students should divide a sheet of construction paper into fourths. In each section, they can quick-sketch what they observe and choose three facts to include under each drawing.

3. Using a video-calling program that has video conferencing, connect with a classroom in the community students have been observing. Let students read their observations to the other class and discuss the culture and lifestyle they have been observing.

4. Use student observations and perceptions for both small- and large-group discussions.

Ideas for Future Lessons

✳ Have students observe animals in zoos or animal sanctuaries and write notes about the relationships between the animals.

✳ Have students watch an ocean Webcam and classify the various fish and plants they see. Have them follow up with online research. Have them organize their findings into an e-scrapbook and upload to the class wiki.

Publishing Student Work

E-portfolios

Portfolios of student work have traditionally been in the form of file folders, notebooks, envelopes, or boxes. An electronic portfolio, or *e-portfolio*, uses technology to store the students' work. You can store text documents, photos, sound recordings, movies, graphics, and hyperlinks in an e-portfolio. Creating e-portfolios enables students to view each other's work. They can also be used for students to reflect back on what they learned.

Types of Electronic Portfolios

* **Working Portfolio** – A collection of student's work, usually arranged with most recent work first and new work added as it is completed. This enables students to reflect back on their work.

* **Presentation Portfolio** – Created for a purpose or audience; the portfolio is the product.

Tips

> There are Web sites designed to help manage student e-portfolios.

> Portfolios can be shared with other classrooms and viewed by parents.

> Joint projects with other teachers can be created, changed, and stored online.

> Students can submit work over time.

> Typical student work to highlight in an e-portfolio are writings, artwork, music, photographs, and videos.

Procedure

The e-portfolios come from an assignment or are an end-of-study collection of work.

1. (For assignment portfolios only) Make a list of what work you want in the portfolio. These pieces can be related projects around a unit of study, they may be outcomes from small-group work, or they may be the requirements to pass a class. In addition to the assignment, you may wish to let students include one piece of work of their own choice.

   (For end-of-study collection only) Have students collect the work they want to share. Make sure they select representations of their best work. Have them write reflections on why they made the choices they did. These can be used as introductions to the work or as a part of the cover page. (See Step 3.)

2. Set up an electronic folder for students to store work. Either name the folders yourself or let students name them. Be sure the e-portfolios are named in such a way to make it easy for the student, the teacher, and the audience to find.

3. Instruct students to make a cover page for the e-portfolio, to serve as an introduction to the reader. It may contain a table of contents and should state the purpose of the portfolio.

4. As work is completed, direct students to store it in the e-portfolio. This is not a place to put drafts—this is for final work. Putting work into the portfolio is a form of publishing, because it will be viewed by an audience.

5. Students should write a page at the end describing what they learned, or they can include a page for each piece that answers the question "What did I learn?"

6. Evaluate e-portfolios by using a rubric or a "pass" or "not yet" evaluation. E-portfolios allow you to track each student's progress.

Teacher Resources

Reliable Web Sites

You will quickly learn that Web sites come and go. This list was compiled with reliability in mind. We cannot guarantee that these sites will remain in existence, but all were reliable at the time of publication of this book.

readwritethink.org

This Web site is produced by the International Reading Association (IRA) and the National Council of Teachers of English (NCTE). It contains classroom lessons, standards, a lengthy list of Web resources, and student materials.

catalog.loc.gov

This Library of Congress online catalog is useful for finding authors, titles, and whether books are in print or not.

www2.scholastic.com

Features pages for teachers with resources, student activities, and book recommendations, as well as pages for kids and parents that include games, book reviews, videos, and message boards.

www.cia.gov/library/publications/the-world-factbook/index.html

This is the Central Intelligence Agency's World Factbook. It contains profiles on every country, flags of the world, and kids' pages on the CIA.

www.nationalgeographic.com

Operated by the National Geographic Society, this site has kids' pages that include videos, activities, games, and stories on cultures around the world.

www.timeforkids.com

This site is operated by *Time* magazine and offers articles and activities for both students and teachers.

bensguide.gpo.gov

This site offers student-friendly explanations of the U.S. Government. It provides links to the U.S. government Web sites for kids and students.

webzero.si.edu/kids

This Web site is run by the Smithsonian and includes many activities for kids and lesson plans for teachers.

factfinder.census.gov/home/en/kids/kids.html

The U.S. Census Bureau offers facts, quizzes, and activities for kids.

www.whitehouse.gov/about/white_house_101

White House tours, presidential facts, and historical information for all ages.

www.nps.gov/learn/home.htm

The National Park Service Web site offers information and links to all the national parks and many teaching resources.

www.weather.com

Operated by the Weather Channel, this site offers worldwide weather news, as well as articles and videos on all kinds of weather.

www.mayoclinic.com

Operated by the Mayo Clinic, this site provides reliable information on diseases and conditions, drugs and supplements, healthy lifestyle, and first aid.

nationalzoo.si.edu

This is the Web site of the Smithsonian National Zoological Park. It includes photo galleries, live cams, and online exhibits.

www.nasa.gov

Offering a wealth of information for educators and for students, the NASA Web sites include articles, news, web-cams, videos, and podcasts.

www.lib.noaa.gov/researchtools/subjectguides/wind/education.html

The National Oceanographic Data Center offers a Teachers and Students Corner with information on climate, water, weather, and sea life, plus links to many related sites.

www.nsf.gov/news/classroom

The National Science Foundation offers a diverse collection of lessons and Web resources for teachers and students in all areas of math and science.

www.howstuffworks.com

Provides quizzes, videos, current events, amazing pictures, and information on a wide range of topics.

pbskids.org

Features activities that go with children's television programs offered on PBS.

kids.discovery.com

Games, activities, and videos on this site go with programs offered on the Discovery Channel.

Other reliable resources:

* Presidential libraries
* University Web sites
* Government agencies
* State departments of education
* Agricultural extension agencies
* Museums and historical sites
* Zoos, planetariums, and aquariums

Glossary

audiobook	a taped recording of a book
bcc (blind carbon copy)	sending an e-mail to multiple people that conceals individual e-mail addresses from the list of recipients
blog	a contraction of the term Weblog; a Web site written in the form of a journal or diary—readers may leave comments in an interactive format
cc (carbon copy)	recipients of a copy of an e-mail
classroom response system (CRS)	a device that allows students to use a remote control to answer questions
digital camera	a camera that records and stores photographic images to be viewed in the camera's memory or uploaded to a computer or printer
download	to copy or move files, programs, or information into a computer's memory, especially from the Internet onto one computer (download means "receive")
DVD (digital versatile disc or digital video disc)	a disc used for storing and playing music, film, or information
e-book (electronic book)	a book published in electronic form and not on paper
E-mail	a message sent over the Internet
e-portfolio (electronic portfolio)	a way to store student work on a computer
LCD projector	a projector that can project video, images, or computer data on a screen or other flat surface
MP3 player	a device for playing music that has been stored electronically
podcast	a radio program that can be played on a computer or MP3 player
search engine	a software program that searches for Web sites by topic
social networking	Web sites where individuals post personal profiles and share information, common interests, photographs, and communicate with select people
spam	unwanted e-mail, usually advertisements
tripod	a three-legged stand used for holding a camera steady

tinyURL	a service that allows users to shorten a long URL into a shorter, easier-to-remember one
tweet	a message sent on Twitter, a social networking service
upload	to copy or move files, programs, or information from a computer to the Internet
URL	a Web site address
video calling	a way of communicating on a computer that is a telephone with video screen
Web site	a place on the Internet with information about a particular subject
Webcam	a camera that broadcasts moving pictures and sound on the Internet as it happens
whiteboard	electronic equipment in the shape of a flat, white board that is connected to a computer; it is written on using a special pen that also controls the computer
wiki	a Web site that allows users to add to or change the posted content

....

Permission Form

Name of Student _____

School _____

Teacher _____ **Grade** _____

As the parent or legal guardian of the minor student listed above, I grant permission for him or her to access networked computer services for participating in teacher-supervised activities to learn about the following digital tools:

(check all that apply)

____ e-mails	____ blogs	____ digital movies	____ other
____ Internet search engines	____ podcasts	____ Webcams	_____
____ wikis	____ digital photographs	____ e-porfolios	_____

Related to these activities, I give my permission to publish my child's: ____ **photo** ____ **writing** ____ **art work**

_____ **I would like further information.** The best times to reach me are _____.

The best contact number is _____.

Parent Signature _____ **Date** _____